VEGETARIAN DISHES & DESSERTS

CONTENTS

D0450189

Ennai Kathirikkai 3	Quzar-e-Pukhtan 39
Vendaka Masala Pachchadi 5	Baingan ka Salan 41
Bisi Bele Huliyana 6	Kadhi 43
Masala Dosa 8	Besan ke Gatte 44
Idli 11	Papad ki Sabzi 47
Muttakos Poriyal 13	Palak Kofta 49
Mirchi ka Salan 15	Paneer Tawa Masala 51
Daal Bukhara 17	Coconut Burfee 52
Vegetable Jalfrezi 19	Kulfi 53
Guncha-o-Keema 21	Moong Daal Halwa 54
Gobhi Taka Tin 23	Saffron Phirni 55
Dhingri Matar Hara Pyaz 25	Kheer 57
Vegetable Korma 27	Gajrela 58
Khud Pukht Qureshi 29	Gulab Jamum 59
Potato Saagu 31	Mint Relish 60
Zanat-e-Numa 33	Saunth 61
Kela Kofta 35	Bhuraani Raita 62
Kadhai Paneer 37	Mixed Raita 63
Karele Masale Wale 38	Sambhar 64

Vegetarianism is a way of life in India and contrary to popular belief, a completely vegetarian meal can be both satisfying and healthy. A typical vegetarian meal generally consists of a lentil or curry dish, complemented by a dry vegetable dish, raita (garnished yoghurt) and pickles with rice and one of a variety of Indian breads. The meal is finished off with a sweet dish followed by paan or betel leaf and betel nuts.

Vegetables, of which a wide variety is available in India, are usually cooked according to the weather. In the hot summer, little oil and few spices are used while in winter, when green leafy vegetables are in abundance, a variety of spices and elaborate cooking can make each meal a gourmet experience. Most of the recipes given in this section can tempt the most devout non-vegetarian to convert.

SERVES: 4

ENNAI KATHIRIKKAI

An unusual dish of stuffed eggplants from the southern part of India.

Ingredients

Small brinjals (eggplants)	1 lb/10 pieces	Curry leaves	10
Asafoetida (*heeng*)	a pinch	Mustard (*sarson*) seeds	⅛ oz/½ tsp
Bengal gram lentils	¼ lb /½ tbs	Red chillies, whole	4
Coconut, grated	5 oz/⅔ cup	Salt to taste	
Cooking oil	2 fl oz/¼ cup	Tamarind (*imlee*) extract	¼ oz/1 tsp
Coriander seeds	½ oz/1 tbs	Yellow (*urad daal*) lentils,	
Cumin (*jeera*) seeds	½ oz/1 tbs	husked and split	½ oz/1 tbs

Method

1. On a hot griddle, roast the grated coconut till golden brown. Remove.

2. Reserve half of both the lentils and broil the other half till light brown.

3. In a blender, make a thick paste of the broiled lentils with the tamarind extract. Use 1-2 tablespoons of water, if necessary.

4. Slit eggplants into four without separating them, leaving them joined at the stem end. Fill with the lentil paste.

5. Heat oil in a pan, add mustard seeds, reserved lentils, curry leaves and asafoetida.

6. When seeds begin to crackle add coriander seeds, cumin seeds and red chillies. Place eggplants in the pan, add salt and left over paste, if any. Add 4 fl oz/½ cup water. Stir carefully for 2-3 minutes, cover and simmer over gentle heat till eggplants are tender.

Note

For variation add chopped tomatoes along with the prepared eggplants.

Tips

Time	**To Serve**
Preparation: 30 minutes	Serve hot with boiled rice
Cooking: 20 minutes	

3

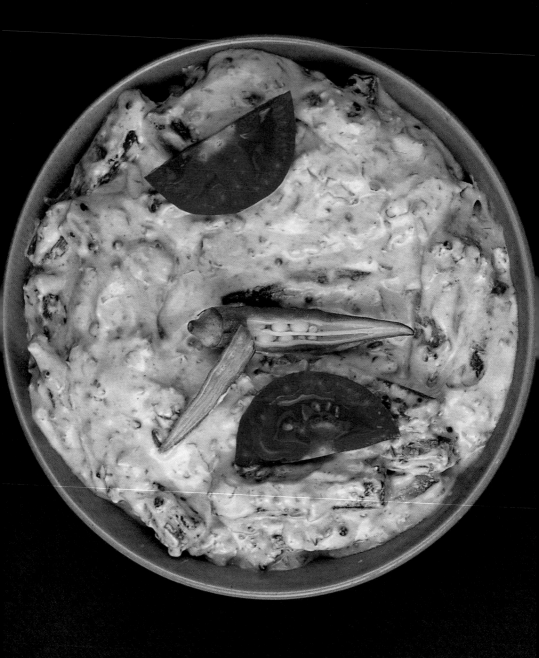

VENDAKA MASALA PACHCHADI

Another coconut flavored fried lady's fingers curry from the South.

Ingredients

Lady's fingers	2 lb	Onions, chopped	4 oz/½ cup
Cashew nuts	½ oz/1 tbs	Red chilli powder	¼ oz/1 tsp
Coconut milk	2 fl oz/¼ cup	Red chillies, whole	3
Coriander powder	½ oz/1 tbs	Salt to taste	
Cumin (*jeera*) seeds	⅛ oz/½ tsp	Tomatoes, chopped	8¾ oz/1 cup
Curry leaves	10	Turmeric (*haldi*) powder	⅛ oz/½ tsp
Grated coconut	2½ oz/⅓ cup	Lentils (*urad daal*)	
Groundnut/peanut oil to deep fry		husked and split	¾ oz/4 tsp
Mustard (*sarson*) seeds	¼ oz/1 tsp	Yoghurt	4 oz/½ cup

Method

1. Wash, pat dry and cut the okra into 1 inch pieces.

2. Heat the groundnut/peanut oil in a kadhai and deep fry the lady's fingers on medium heat till crisp, about 5-6 minutes. Drain and reserve the oil.

3. Put the cashew nuts and the coconut in a blender, add coconut milk and make a fine paste.

4. Heat 2½ fl oz of the reserved oil, add cumin and mustard seeds, urad daal, whole red chillies and the curry leaves. Sauté over medium heat till the seeds begin to crackle. Add onions. Sauté till golden brown.

5. Stir in the tomatoes, then add red chilli powder, turmeric, coriander and salt. Keep stirring till the fat separates.

6. Reduce the flame, add the coconut paste and stir again for 2 minutes. Remove from the fire and add yoghurt. Stir, add 13 fl oz/ 1⅔ cups water. Return to heat and bring to boil. Simmer.

7. Add the deep fried lady's fingers and cook till gravy seeps in.

Tips

Time	To Serve
Preparation: 30 minutes Cooking: 30 minutes	Transfer to a shallow dish and serve with boiled rice

SERVES: 4

BISI BELE HULIYANA

A delicious South Indian dish of hot and sour rice and lentils cooked together.

Ingredients

Basmati rice	10¾ oz/1¼ cups	Green peas	2 oz/¼ cup
Lentils (*toor daal*)	5 oz/⅔ cup	Groundnut/peanut oil to deep fry 1 fl oz/2
Asafoetida (*heeng*)	⅛ oz/½ tsp	tbs	
Cardamoms	5	Groundnut/peanut oil for tempering1 fl oz/
Cashew nuts, split	¾ oz/4 tsp	2 tbs	
Cauliflower, small florets	2 oz/¼ cup	Lentils (*urad daal*),	
Bengal gram		husked and split	1 oz/2 tbs
(*chana daal*), husked		Mustard (*sarson*) seeds	⅛ oz/½ tsp
and split	2 oz/¼ cup	Red chilli powder	⅛ oz/½ tsp
Cinnamon	2 sticks of 1" each	Red chillies, whole	2
Cloves	5	Salt to taste	
Cumin (*jeera*) seeds	¼ oz/1 tsp	Tamarind (*imlee*) extract	1½ oz/3 tbs
Curry leaves	10	Tomatoes, chopped	14 oz/1⅔ cups
Fenugreek (*methi*) seeds	¼ oz/1 tsp	Turmeric (*haldi*) powder	¼ oz/1 tsp

Method

1. Wash rice and toor daal and soak seperately for 30 minutes.

2. To make the masala, broil the gram and urad daal separately on a griddle till light brown.

3. Broil the cinnamon, cardamoms, cloves, cumin seeds and fenugreek seeds separately on the griddle for 30 seconds each. Grind together with the broiled urad daal and gram in a blender.

4. Deep fry the cashew nuts till golden brown. Keep aside.

5. Put toor daal in a handi, add 2.5 litres/10 cups water and bring to a boil. Let simmer until almost cooked.

6. Drain rice and add to the daal with peas and cauliflower and simmer for 10 minutes. Stir occasionally.

7. Stir in the tomatoes, tamarind and the asafoetida.

8. Add red chilli powder, turmeric and salt. Stir in the blended masala.

9. Cover and simmer till lentils and rice are mashed and achieve a porridge like consistency.

10. Sprinkle curry leaves and let simmer.

11. Meanwhile, heat 1 fl oz/2 tablespoons oil in a kadhai and crackle mustard seeds in it. Add whole red chillies and stir for 15 seconds.

12. Pour the tempering over the lentil-rice mixture. Stir for 2 minutes.

Tips

Time	To Serve
Preparation: 40 minutes Cooking: 40 minutes	Garnish with cashew nuts and serve with mango pickle and poppadams

MASALA DOSA

SERVES: 4

*A variety of fillings can be stuffed into the dosa
to make it a wholesome meal.*

For dosa

Parboiled rice	½ lb
Lentils (*urad daal*), husked and split	6 oz/¾ cup
Fenugreek (*methi*) seeds	⅛ oz/½ tsp
Groundnut/peanut oil	2½ fl oz/⅓ cup
Salt to taste	

For masala

Potatoes, boiled and mashed	8¾ oz/1 cup
Butter	1 oz/2 tbs

Bengal gram (*chana daal*), husked and split	½ oz/1 tbs
Cashew nuts, deep fried	12
Coriander leaves, chopped	¾ oz/4 tsp
Curry leaves	10
Green chillies, chopped	4
Groundnut/peanut oil	2 fl oz/4 tbs
Lemon juice	½ fl oz/1 tbs
Mustard (*sarson*) seeds	¼ oz/1 tsp
Onions, sliced	4 oz/½ cup
Salt to taste	
Turmeric (*haldi*) powder	¼ oz/1 tsp

1. To make the batter for dosas, soak the rice and lentils overnight with the fenugreek seeds. Put in a blender with 1½ fl oz/3 tablespoons water and make a fine paste. Remove to a large container and keep aside in a warm place for 3-4 hours; in winter for 5-6 hours.

2. To make the masala, heat oil in a kadhai, crackle mustard seeds in it, add gram and stir until light brown.

3. Stir in onions and sauté until transparent. Stir in green chillies, turmeric and salt. Add lemon juice.

4. Add potatoes and stir-cook for 5 minutes.

5. Add cashew nuts, curry leaves and coriander.

6. To make the dosas, heat the griddle. Peel an onion and chop into two halves. Tie one half in a muslin cloth, dip in oil and wipe griddle with the flat side to season griddle. This needs to be done only once. Keep griddle on low heat. Spread a ladleful of batter over the entire surface thinly by moving the ladle in concentric circles.

7. Once tiny holes appear on the pancake, sprinkle a teaspoon of oil around the edges and loosen the pancake from the griddle.

8. Slap 2 large tablespoons of the masala filling onto one half of the dosa, drop a knob of butter on it and fold the other half over. Slide off onto a plate.

Variation

Paneer or cottage cheese can be used instead of potatoes as a filling.

Time

Preparation: Overnight plus 6½ hours
Cooking: 25 minutes for masala plus 2-3 minutes for each dosa

To Serve

Serve immediately with coconut chutney and sambhar. For recipes see pp. 11 and 64

SERVES: 4

IDLI

A really light and healthy breakfast dish or snack.

Ingredients

Lentils (*urad daal*),		Coconut, grated	5 oz/⅔ cup
split and husked	5 oz/⅔ cup	Curry leaves	8
Parboiled rice	12¾ oz/1½ cups	Ginger, chopped	½ oz/1 tbs
Oil to grease moulds		Green chillies, chopped	5
Salt to taste		Lentils (*urad daal*)	¼ oz/1 tsp
		Mustard (*sarson*) seeds	¼ oz/1 tsp
For coconut chutney		Oil	½ fl oz/1 tbs
Cashew nuts or		Salt to taste	
Gram (*chana*), roasted	½ oz/1 tbs		

Method

1. Soak lentils for one hour then put in a blender with very little water to obtain a paste slightly thicker in consistency than pancake batter.

2. Coarsely grind rice, then wash and soak for 10 minutes.

3. Put the rice flour in a muslin cloth and squeeze out the moisture.

4. Mix the lentil paste with rice flour and salt and set aside for 6 hours to ferment.

5. Grease idli moulds, fill half-way up with batter and steam in a pressure cooker for 8-10 minutes. A needle inserted in an idli should come out clean if the idli is cooked. If no moulds are available then use small, heat proof bowls and steam in a double boiler or egg poacher.

For coconut chutney

1. Grind coconut, green chillies, ginger and cashew nuts/roasted gram to a paste.

2. Heat oil in a kadhai. Add mustard seeds, urad daal and sauté over medium heat. Add curry leaves.

3. Add the ground paste to the tempering. Heat through.

Time
Preparation: 8½ hours for idlis and 15 minutes for the chutney
Cooking: 8-10 minutes for the idlis and 5 minutes for the chutney

To Serve
Demould idlis and place on individual plates. Serve with coconut chutney and sambhar. For recipe see p. 64

11

MUTTAKOS PORIYAL

A South Indian dish. All poriyals are made in oil and tempered with mustard seeds,
urad daal and red chilli powder and finished with grated coconut.

Ingredients

Cabbage, chopped	1 lb	Mustard (*sarson*) seeds	⅛ oz/½ tsp
Asafoetida (*heeng*)	a pinch	Peas, shelled	5 oz/⅔ cup
Coconut, grated	1 oz/2 tbs	Red chilli, whole	1
Cooking oil	1½ fl oz/3 tbs	Salt to taste	
Cumin (*jeera*) seeds	⅛ oz/½ tsp	Yellow lentils (*urad daal*),	
Curry leaves	10	husked and split	¼ oz/1 tsp
Green chillies, slit	2		

Method

1 Heat oil in a kadhai. Add mustard seeds, cumin seeds, lentils, whole red chilli, asafoetida and the curry leaves.
2. Once mustard seeds crackle add green chillies, cabbage, peas and salt.
3. Stir, cover and cook over gentle heat till vegetables are tender.

Note
Other vegetable like carrots, beetroot or cauliflower can be used instead of the green ones used in this recipe.

Tips

Time
Preparation: 20 minutes
Cooking: 30 minutes

To Serve
Sprinkle with grated coconut and serve hot with parathas.

MIRCHI KA SALAN

It may sound incredible but this dish is cooked to spice up green chillies.

Ingredients

Green chillies	½ lb	Mustard oil (*sarson ka tel*)	4 fl oz/½ cup
Potatoes, peeled and diced	5 oz/⅔ cup	Poppy seeds (*khus khus*)	¼ oz/1 tsp
Coconut, dessicated	1 oz/2 tbs	Red chilli powder	¼ oz/1 tsp
Coriander seeds	¼ oz/1 tsp	Salt to taste	
Cumin (*jeera*) seeds	½ oz/1 tbs	Sesame (*til*) seeds	¼ oz/1 tsp
Curry leaves	10	Tamarind (*imlee*)	1½ oz/6 tsp
Garlic paste	¼ oz/1 tsp	Turmeric (*haldi*) powder	¼ oz/1 tsp
Ginger paste	¼ oz/1 tsp		

Method

1. Roast coriander, cumin, poppy and sesame seeds on a griddle and pound. Roast coconut too.

2. Wash and soak tamarind in 8 fl oz/1 cup water. Mash well, then squeeze out and discard pulp.

3. Remove stem, slit and deseed chillies without separating them. Pat dry.

4. Heat oil in a kadhai. Fry potatoes till golden brown. Remove. Reserve a few green chillies for garnish. Fry the rest till soft. Drain.

5. In the same oil brown the ginger and garlic pastes, ground seeds, turmeric, chilli powder, curry leaves and coconut. Add green chillies and 16 fl oz/2 cups water. Cover and simmer for 5 minutes.

6. Add fried potatoes and simmer till chillies and potatoes are tender.

7. Add tamarind juice through a stainer and let simmer till gravy thickens.

Tips

Time	**To Serve**
Preparation: 20 minutes	Garnish with slit green chillies and
Cooking: 30 minutes	serve with plain boiled rice

DAAL BUKHARA

Black lentils cooked over a slow fire for hours on end are a favorite with almost all gourmets. The dish tastes best after being stored in the refrigerator overnight and reheated.

Ingredients

Black lentils, whole		Ginger paste	¾ oz/4 tsp
(*urad daal*)	10¾ oz/1¼ cups	Salt to taste	
Chilli powder	¼ oz/1 tsp	Tomato purée	5 fl oz/⅔ cup
Cream	5 fl oz/⅔ cup	White butter	4 oz/½ cup
Garlic paste	¾ oz/4 tsp		

Method

1. Pick, clean and soak daal for at least 3 hours; best soaked overnight.
2. Add 6 cups water to the daal and cook over a low flame till grain splits and daal is mashed. It is traditionally cooked over charcoal embers for 6 hours or overnight with 64 fl oz/8 cups of water. It can also be cooked for 12 hours in a slow cooker.

3. Stir the lentils vigorously to mash them.
4. Add the tomato purée, ginger and garlic pastes, salt and chilli powder and cook for an hour till daal is thick.
5. Keep aside 2 tsp butter and add the rest to the daal along with the cream and cook for another 15 minutes, stirring continuously till the fat is incorporated into the daal.

Tips

Time	To Serve
Preparation: overnight	Add the reserved butter and serve hot with tandoori roti or naan. For recipes see pp. 63 and 64 of the ***Tandoor & Dry Dishes*** section
Cooking: 2½ hours on a gas stove; overnight on charcoal or a slow cooker.	

VEGETABLE JALFREZI

An easy to make, delightfully quick vegetable mix.

Ingredients

Beans	4 oz	Onion	4 oz
Cabbage	4 oz	Pepper powder	$^1/_8$ oz/$^1/_2$ tsp
Capsicum	4 oz	Potato fingers	4 oz
Carrots	4 oz	Red chillies, whole	2
Cooking oil	2 fl oz/4 tbs	Salt to taste	
Coriander leaves, chopped	$^1/_2$ oz/1 tbs	Tomato purée	2 fl oz/4 tbs
Cumin (*jeera*) seeds	$^1/_4$ oz/1 tsp	White vinegar	$^1/_2$ fl oz/1 tbs
Ginger, chopped	$^1/_4$ oz/1 tsp		

Method

1. Wash and chop all vegetables, except potatoes.
2. Heat oil in a pan. Add the cumin and whole red chillies and sauté.
3. Add all the vegetables, salt, pepper and ginger. Stir well. Cover with lid and cook on slow fire till almost tender.
4. Add tomato purée and white vinegar. Cook till done.
5. Remove from fire.

Time
Preparation: 45 minutes
Cooking: 30 minutes

To Serve
Garnish with chopped coriander. Serve with any Indian bread

GUNCHA-O-KEEMA

This is a rich, crispy, cauliflower preparation.

Ingredients

Cauliflower florets	1¼ lb	Garlic, chopped	¾ oz/4 tsp
Butter	4 oz/½ cup	Ginger juliennes	¼ oz/1 tsp
Green pepper, diced	1 oz/2 tbs	Juice of 1 lemon	
Chaat masala	⅛ oz/½ tsp	Khoya	2 oz/4 tbs
Chilli powder	¼ oz/1 tsp	Salt to taste	
Cooking oil	½ fl oz/1 tbs	Tomato purée	2 fl oz/4 tbs
Coriander leaves, chopped	¼ oz/1 tsp	Tomatoes, diced	1 oz/2 tbs
Garam masala	⅛ oz/½ tsp	Turmeric (*haldi*) powder	⅛ oz/½ tsp

Method

1. Heat cooking oil in a kadhai. Sauté garlic. Add cauliflower, turmeric, chilli powder and salt.
2. Cook on low flame till cauliflower is almost tender. Remove and keep aside.
3. In another pan melt butter and toss the green pepper and diced tomatoes in it. Add to the cooked cauliflower. In the same pan brown the khoya till it becomes granulated.
4. Add tomato purée to the cauliflower and cook for a minute. Sprinkle with khoya granules, chaat masala, garam masala and lemon juice.

Time
Preparation: 20 minutes
Cooking: 45 minutes

To Serve
Garnish with ginger juliennes and coriander leaves. Serve hot with any Indian bread

GOBHI TAKA TIN

Fried cauliflower, cooked with green pepper and tomato in masala.

Ingredients

Cauliflower	1 lb	Ginger paste	1½ oz/3 tbs
Green pepper, cubed	3¼ oz/1 large	Dry fenugreek leaves	¼ oz/1 tsp
Coriander leaves, chopped	½ oz/1 tbs	Oil	5 fl oz/⅔ cup
Cumin (*jeera*) powder	¼ oz/1 tsp	Onions, chopped	6 oz/¾ cup
Cumin (*jeera*) seeds	⅛ oz/½ tsp	Red chilli powder	¾ oz/4 tsp
Garam masala	½ oz/1 tbs	Salt to taste	
Garlic paste	1½ oz/3 tbs	Tomatoes, cubed	8¾ oz/1 cup
Green chillies, chopped	1 oz/8	Yoghurt	4 oz/½ cup
Ginger juliennes	¼ oz/1 tsp		

Method

1. Break the cauliflower into small florets.
2. Heat oil in a kadhai. Fry the cauliflower and keep aside.
3. In the same oil add cumin seeds. When they begin to crackle add chopped onions. Fry till golden brown.
4. Add the ginger and garlic pastes, green chillies, salt, chilli powder, cumin powder, garam masala, kasoori methi and yoghurt. Stir-fry.
5. Add green pepper and tomato cubes and fry again.
6. Add cauliflower and simmer for 5 minutes.

Time
Preparation: 25 minutes
Cooking: 25 minutes

To Serve
Garnish with coriander leaves and ginger juliennes. Serve hot

DHINGRI MATAR HARA PYAZ

An easy to cook yet delicious mixture of vegetables.

Ingredients

Button mushrooms	2 lb	Garlic, chopped	1 oz/2 tbs
Green peas, shelled	4 oz	Onions, sliced	4 oz/½ cup
Spring onions	4 oz	Red chilli powder	⅛ oz/½ tsp
Almond paste	1 oz/2 tbs	Salt to taste	
Cooking oil	2½ fl oz/⅓ cup	Tomato purée	8 fl oz/1 cup
Garam masala	¼ oz/1 tsp		

Method

1. Trim, wash and quarter mushrooms.

2. Boil peas till tender, drain and keep aside.

3. Slice spring onions. Chop the green stems of the onions finely for garnishing and keep aside.

4. Heat oil in a saucepan and sauté chopped garlic till brown. Add sliced onions and sauté till golden brown. Add salt, chilli powder, tomato purée and 8 fl oz/1 cup water and cook for a minute.

5. Remove from fire and strain gravy through a soup strainer into another saucepan.

6. Put back on fire and cook till almost all the liquid has evaporated and the masala is sizzling.

7. Add mushrooms and spring onions and cook for 5 minutes. Add the peas and simmer till mushrooms are done.

8. Stir in the almond paste and cook till the gravy reaches a sauce-like consistency.

Time

Preparation: 30 minutes
Cooking: 30 minutes

To Serve

Garnish with spring onion greens. Serve hot with roti or naan. For recipes see pp. 63 and 64 of the ***Tandoor & Dry Dishes*** section

VEGETABLE KORMA

A mixed vegetable delight with the goodness of many fresh vegetables in one dish.

Ingredients

Beans, chopped	3 oz	Cloves	3
Carrots, diced	3 oz	Coconut, grated	5 oz/²⁄₃ cup
Kohlrabi, dried	3 oz	Coriander leaves, chopped	¼ oz/1 tsp
Peas, shelled	3 oz	Fennel (*saunf*)	¼ oz/1 tsp
Potatoes, diced	3 oz	Ginger, chopped	¼ oz/1 tsp
Tomatoes, chopped	3 oz	Green chillies, chopped	2
Bay leaf (*tej patta*)	2	Onions, chopped	1 oz/2 tbs
Cardamoms	6	Poppy seeds (*khus khus*)	¼ oz/1 tsp
Cinnamon	1" stick	Salt to taste	
Clarified butter (*ghee*)	1 oz/2 tbs	Turmeric (*haldi*) powder	¹⁄₈ oz/½ tsp

Method

1. Blend coconut, green chillies, onions, ginger, turmeric powder and coriander leaves to a fine past in a blender.

2. On a hot griddle roast the fennel, cinnamon, cloves, cardamoms and poppy seeds. Cool and put in a blender to make a fine powder.

3. In a pan put just enough water to cover the vegetables along with bay leaves and salt and cook.

4. Once the vegetables are tender and the water evaporated add the coconut-onion paste. Stir-cook for 2-3 minutes.

5. Add the powdered seeds and clarified butter. Stir well for 5 minutes.

Tips

Time
Preparation: 45 minutes
Cooking takes 30 minutes

To Serve
Transfer to a dish and serve with roti.

KHUD PUKHT QURESHI

A smooth lentil delicacy from the kitchen of the Mughal kings.

Ingredients

Lentils *(arhar daal)*	8¾ oz/1 cup	Onions, chopped	4 oz/½ cup
Butter or clarified		Pepper to taste	
butter *(ghee)*	4 oz/½ cup	Red chillies, whole	4
Cream	4 oz/½ cup	Salt to taste	
Cumin *(jeera)* seeds	⅛ oz/½ tsp	Red chilli powder	¼ oz/1 tsp
Garlic, chopped	½ oz/1 tbs	Yoghurt	8¾ oz/1 cup
Garlic paste	½ oz/1 tbs		

Method

1. Pick and wash lentils. Boil with 32 fl oz/ 4 cups water, salt and red chilli powder till tender.

2. Add garlic paste and cook for a further 10 minutes.

3. Add the cream and yoghurt and 2 oz/ ¼ cup butter. Cook again for 10 minutes, stiring frequently so that the fat is incorporated into the daal.

4. Heat remaining half of the butter in a pan. Sauté the chopped garlic, cumin and onions for 2 minutes. Add whole red chillies and sauté till brown. Add to the cooked lentils.

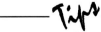

Time
Preparation: 15 minutes
Cooking: 30 minutes

To Serve
Serve hot with a knob of butter and roti. For recipe see p. 63 of the ***Tandoor & Dry Dishes*** section

POTATO SAAGU

A spicy potato delicacy in a thick curry.

Ingredients

Potatoes	2.2 lb	Ginger, chopped	¼ oz/1 tsp
Asafoetida (*heeng*)	a pinch	Gram (*chana*), roasted	1 oz/2 tbs
Black peppercorns	¼ oz/1 tsp	Green chillies	2
Cinnamon	1" stick	Mustard (*sarson*) seeds	¼ oz/1 tsp
Cloves	2	Onions, chopped	1 oz/2 tbs
Coconut, grated	1 oz/2 tbs	Red chillies, whole	2
Cooking oil	1½ fl oz/3 tbs	Salt to taste	
Coriander leaves, chopped	¼ oz/1 tsp	Tomatoes, chopped	1 oz/2 tbs
Cumin (*jeera*) seeds	¼ oz/1 tsp	Turmeric (*haldi*) powder	¼ oz/1 tsp
Curry leaves	6		

Method

1. Wash, peel and dice potatoes in half inch cubes.

2. Make a paste of the green chillies, roasted gram, cumin seeds, black peppercorns, ginger, cinnamon, cloves and grated coconut with a little water in a blender.

3. Heat oil in a kadhai. Add asafoetida, mustard seeds, whole red chillies and curry leaves.

4. When mustard seeds start to splutter add onions and sauté lightly. Add turmeric, stir and add tomatoes. Stir for 2-3 minutes.

5. Add potatoes, salt and sufficient water to cover potatoes. Cover and simmer till tender.

6. Add the prepared paste and simmer gently for 4-5 minutes.

Note

Saagu can also be made with mixed vegetables.

Tips

Time
Preparation: 30 minutes
Cooking: 45 minutes

To Serve
Garnish with chopped coriander. Serve hot with paratha. For recipe see p. 61 of the ***Tandoor & Dry Dishes*** section

ZANAT-E-NUMA

This stuffed potato curry is as exotic as its popular name.

Ingredients

Potatoes	2.2 lb	Green chillies	10
Clarified butter (*ghee*)	1 oz/2 tbs	Mint	1½ oz/3 tbs
Cooking oil for gravy	3 fl oz/6 tbs	Raisins	¾ oz/4 tsp
Cooking oil to deep fry		Red chilli powder	¼ oz/1 tsp
Coriander leaves	3 oz/6 tbs	Salt to taste	
Coriander powder	¼ oz/1 tsp	Spinach	14 oz
Cumin (*jeera*) seeds	⅛ oz/½ tsp	Tomatoes, chopped	2½ oz/⅓ cup
Dry mango powder (*amchur*)	¼ oz/1 tsp	Turmeric (*haldi*) powder	⅛ oz/½ tsp
Fenugreek (*methi*), fresh	3½ oz/7 tbs	Yoghurt	1½ oz/3 tbs
Garam masala	¼ oz/1 tsp		

Method

1. Take medium sized, rounded potatoes. Peel and scoop out the centre then deep fry the shell.

2. Grind mint, coriander leaves, green chillies, cumin, mango powder, raisins and salt with very little water into a chutney (relish) and set aside.

3. Heat 3 fl oz/6 tablespoons oil in a kadhai. Add turmeric powder, tomatoes, spinach and fenugreek leaves. Sauté lightly.

4. Add red chilli powder and salt and cook till gravy thickens. Add the yoghurt, garam masala, coriander powder and clarified butter.

5. Remove from heat and push through a thick sieve. Set aside.

6. Stuff the potatoes with the mint and coriander chutney.

7. Place the potatoes in a shallow dish and pour the hot strained gravy over.

Tips

Time
Preparation: 45 minutes
Cooking: 1 hour

To Serve
Serve immediately with biryani.

SERVES: 4

KELA KOFTA

Fried raw banana dumplings in a thick aromatic gravy.

Ingredients

Raw bananas	1 lb	Green chillies	6
Cardamoms	6	Honey	¼ fl oz/1 tsp
Cinnamon	1" stick	Mace (*javitri*) powder	a pinch
Cloves	4	Oil to deep fry	
Coriander leaves, chopped	¾ oz/4 tsp	Onions, chopped fine	2 oz/¼ cup
Cream	2 fl oz/¼ cup	Onions, chopped	2 oz/¼ cup
Dough for sealing dish		Red chilli powder	¼ oz/1 tsp
Garlic paste	½ oz/1 tbs	Salt to taste	
Ginger, chopped fine	½ oz/1 tbs	Tomatoes, chopped	5 oz/⅔ cup
Ginger paste	½ oz/1 tbs	White pepper powder	⅛ oz/½ tsp

Method

1. Put bananas in a pan, cover with water and boil for 30 minutes. Cool, peel and mash.
2. Mix in the finely chopped onion, ginger, coriander, green chillies, white pepper powder and salt. Divide into 15 portions and roll into balls (koftas) between your palms. Deep fry in a kadhai over low heat till golden brown. Keep aside.
3. Remove excess oil from the kadhai, leaving behind 4 tablespoons. Heat oil and crackle cardamoms, cloves and cinnamon in it. Add the roughly chopped onions. Sauté till transparent.•Add ginger and garlic pastes and sauté till onions turn brown.

4. Make a purée of the tomatoes in a blender.
5. Add tomato purée, red chilli powder and salt to the kadhai. Stir-cook till oil separate.
6. Add 13 fl oz/1⅔ cups water. Bring to boil, remove and strain through soup strainer into another pot.
7. Put the pot on fire and bring gravy to boil. Add cream. Remove and add honey.
8. Arrange koftas in an oven proof casserole. Pour gravy over, sprinkle with mace powder, cover and seal dish with dough.
9. Place dish in preheated oven at 275 °F for 8-10 minutes.

Tips

Time
Preparation: 45 minutes
Cooking: 45 minutes

To Serve
Open the seal and serve with boiled rice or paratha.

KADHAI PANEER

Cottage cheese takes the place of a non-vegetarian dish in an Indian vegetarian menu.
*This hot **Kadhai Paneer** dish is an all time, colorful favorite.*

Ingredients

Cottage cheese (*paneer*)	1¼ lb	Green chillies, chopped	4
Capsicum juliennes	¾ oz	Groundnut/peanut oil	4 fl oz/½ cup
Coriander seeds	½ oz/3 tsp	Dry fenugreek leaves (*methi*)	¼ oz/1 tsp
Corinader leaves, chopped	½ oz/3 tsp	Red chillies, whole	15
Garam masala	¼ oz/1 tsp	Salt to taste	
Garlic paste	¼ oz/1 tsp	Tomatoes, chopped	1½ lb/2¾ cups
Ginger, chopped	1 oz/2 tbs		

Method

1. Pound the red chillies and coriander seeds into a powder.

2. Heat 2½ fl oz/5 tablespoons oil in a kadhai, add garlic paste and sauté till light brown.

3. Add half the pounded spices. Sauté for 30 seconds. Stir in green chillies and ginger, sauté for 30 seconds.

4. Add tomatoes and stir-cook till the fat surfaces.

5. Add dry fenugreek leaves methi, salt and garam masala. Set aside.

6. In another pan heat the remaining 1¼ fl oz/2⅓ tablespoons oil. Add the capsicum and sauté for 30 seconds.

7. Add the remaining pounded coriander and red chilli powder. Stir for 30 seconds. Stir in the cooked masala, reduce flame and stir-cook till fat surfaces.

8. Slice the cottage cheese into fingers and add. Stir gently for 2-3 minutes. Sprinkle chopped coriander.

Time
Preparation: 15 minutes
Cooking: 30 minutes

To Serve
Remove to a serving bowl and serve hot with paratha or naan. For recipes see pp. 61 and 64 of the **Tandoor & Dry Dishes** section

KARELE MASALE WALE

Start with small quantities of the vegetable to acquire the taste. Its blood cleansing qualities make it popular.

Ingredients

Bitter gourd	2.2 lb		Red chilli powder	¹/₈ oz/¹/₂ tsp
Black pepper powder	¹/₈ oz/¹/₂ tsp		Salt for rubbing	1¹/₂ oz/3 tbs
Dry mango powder (*amchur*)	¹/₄ oz/1 tsp		Salt to taste	
Oil to shallow fry	4 fl oz/¹/₂ cup		String to tie the gourds	
Onions, chopped	1 lb/1¾ cups		Turmeric (*haldi*) powder	¹/₈ oz/¹/₂ tsp

Method

1. Wash, scrape and make long slits on one side of the bitter gourds. Reserve scrapings.
2. Rub 2 tablespoons salt on gourds and mix 1 tablespoon salt with scrapings. Keep in the sun for half an hour.
3. Squeeze gourds and scrapings between palms to remove as much moisture as possible. This reduces the bitterness of the gourd.
4. Reserve one fourth of the chopped onions. Mix the rest with the mango powder, black pepper, red chillies and turmeric.
5. Stuff this mixture in the gourds. Wrap string firmly round the gourds so that they do not lose their shape in cooking.
6. Heat oil in a pan and shallow fry the gourds, turning over constantly to ensure all sides are done. Remove.
7. In the remaining oil shallow fry any left over filling, onions, and scrapings.
8. Return gourds to pan. Stir for a minute.

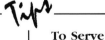

SERVES: 4

QUZAR-E-PUKHTAN

Cottage cheese cubes in spicy tomato purée.

Ingredients

Cottage cheese (*paneer*), in 1" cubes	2 lb	Coriander leaves, chopped	¼ oz/1 tsp
Tomatoes, quartered	½ lb	Garam masala	¼ oz/1 tsp
Black cumin		Garlic paste	1½ oz/3 tbs
(*shah jeera*) seeds	a pinch	Ginger paste	1½ oz/3 tbs
Butter	4 oz/½ cup	Mace (*javitri*) powder	a pinch
Cardamom powder	⅛ oz/½ tsp	Processed cheese, grated	4 oz/½ cup
Coriander powder	¼ oz/1 tsp	Red chilli powder	¼ oz/1 tsp
		Salt to taste	

Method

1. Put the tomatoes in a pan with very little water and cook till they are well mashed. Add salt, red chillies, ginger and garlic pastes. Cook for 10 minutes then remove from fire, cool and push through a strainer.
2. Melt butter in a pan. Sauté the paneer. Add black cumin and after it crackles pour the tomato extract over the paneer.
3. Sprinkle with garam masala, coriander powder and mace powder.
4. Add grated processed cheese. Bring to boil and simmer for 5 minutes on a slow fire.

Time	To Serve
Preparation: 20 minutes Cooking: 30 minutes	Garnish with chopped coriander and cardamom powder. Serve with naan.

BAINGAN KA SALAN

This eggplant dish is prepared from exotic herbs and spices.

Ingredients

Eggplants (aubergine)	1 lb/8 small	Mustard oil (*sarson ka tel*)	4 fl oz/½ cup
Coconut, dessicated	1¼ oz/7 tsp	Red chilli powder	¼ oz/1 tsp
Coriander seeds	¼ oz/1 tsp	Salt to taste	
Cumin (*jeera*) seeds	¼ oz/1 tsp	Sesame (*til*) seeds	¼ oz/1 tsp
Curry leaves	10	Tamarind (*imlee*)	½ oz/3 tsp
Garlic paste	¼ oz/1 tsp	Turmeric (*haldi*) powder	¼ oz/1 tsp
Ginger paste	¼ oz/1 tsp		

Method

1. Roast coriander, cumin, poppy and seasame seeds on a griddle then pound. Roast coconut too.

2. Wash and soak tamarind in 8 fl oz/1 cup warm water. After 10 minutes, mash well, squeeze and discard pulp. Keep juice aside.

3. Slit eggplants about three-fourths of the length without separating them at the stem end.

4. Heat oil in a kadhai. Fry the eggplants lightly. Remove.

5. In the same oil brown the ginger and garlic pastes, ground spices, turmeric, red chilli powder, curry leaves and coconut.

6. Stir occasionally. Add a little water if masala begins to burn.

7. Add the eggplants and 16 fl oz/2 cups water. Simmer for 10 minutes.

8. Add tamarind juice through a strainer and simmer till gravy thickens.

Time	To Serve
Preparation: 20 minutes Cooking: 30 minutes	Serve with plain boiled rice or an Indian bread

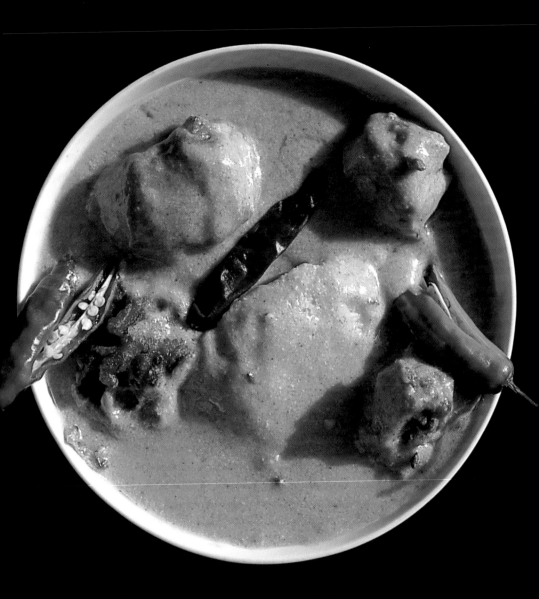

SERVES: 4

KADHI

A tangy, yoghurt and gram flour based gravy with gram flour dumplings floating in it.

Ingredients

Yoghurt	12¾ oz/1½ cups	Onion rounds (¼ " thick)	5 oz
Gram flour (*besan*)	4 oz/½ cup	Potatoes, cut round	5 oz
Carom (*ajwain*) seeds	⅛ oz/½ tsp	Red chilli powder	¼ oz/1 tsp
Cumin (*jeera*) seeds	⅛ oz/½ tsp	Red chillies, whole	4
Fenugreek (*methi*) seeds	a pinch	Salt to taste	
Green chillies, chopped	5	Soda bi-carb	a pinch
Groundnut/peanut oil	2 fl oz/4 tbs	Turmeric (*haldi*) powder	¼ oz/1 tsp
Mustard (*sarson*) seeds	a pinch		
Oil to deep fry			

Method

1. Whip yoghurt, salt, red chilli powder, turmeric and half the gram flour together in a bowl. Keep aside.

2. Sift the other half of the gram flour and soda bi-carb together, add the carom seeds and mix enough water to make a thick batter. Beat well.

3. Add green chillies.

4. Heat enough oil in a kadhai to deep fry. Drop large spoonfuls of the batter in the oil to get 1½ inch puffy dumplings.

5. Fry till golden brown on both sides. Remove and keep aside.

6. Heat 1½ fl oz/3 tablespoons oil in a handi, add the yoghurt mixture and 24 fl oz/3 cups water. Bring to a boil, reduce to a low heat and simmer for 8-10 minutes, stirring constantly to avoid the yoghurt from curdling.

7. Add the potatoes and onions and cook till potatoes are done.

8. Add the dumplings and simmer for 3 minutes.

9. Heat the remaining ½ fl oz/1 tablespoon oil in a small frying pan. Add the cumin, mustard and fenugreek seeds and sauté till the cumin crackles. Add the whole red chillies. Stir.

10. Pour this tempering over the simmering hot kadhi.

Tips

Time
Preparation: 45 minutes
Cooking: 30 minutes

To Serve
Remove to a bowl and serve with boiled rice

BESAN KE GATTE

A hot Rajasthani speciality which has gram flour dumplings in a gravy.

Ingredients

Gram flour	10¾ oz/1¼ cups	Green chillies, chopped	4
Asafoetida (*heeng*)	a large pinch	Mint, chopped	¼ oz/1 tsp
Bay leaves (*tej patta*)	2	Oil to deep fry	
Cinnamon	2 sticks of 1" each	Oil for gravy	4 fl oz/½ cup
Cloves	6	Red chilli powder	¼ oz/1 tsp
Coriander leaves, chopped	½ oz/1 tbs	Salt to taste	
Coriander powder	¾ oz/4 tsp	Soda bi-carb	a pinch
Cumin (*jeera*) seeds	¼ oz/1 tsp	Turmeric (*haldi*) powder	⅛ oz/½ tsp
Garam masala	⅛ oz/½ tsp	Yoghurt	10¾ oz/1¼ cup
Ginger, chopped	½ oz/3 tsp		

Method

1. Mix ginger and half the mint with 2 oz/¼ cup yoghurt and whip.

2. Add ¼ cup oil, gram flour, ¼ oz/1 teaspoon cumin seeds, half the red chilli powder, soda bi-carb and some warm water and knead into a hard, but pliable dough. Divide into 8 and roll into 6 to 8 inch cylinders with the palms.

3. Heat 48 fl oz/6 cups water in a handi. Bring to boil, add the cylinders and boil for 20 minutes.

4. Remove cylinders and set liquid aside. Once the cylinders are cool cut into half inch pieces.

5. Heat oil in a kadhai and deep fry the pieces till golden brown. These are called 'gatte'.

6. Whip the remaining yoghurt in a bowl, add coriander powder, the left over red chilli powder, turmeric and salt. Set aside for 10 minutes.

7. Meanwhile, heat 1½ fl oz/3 tablespoons oil. Crackle the left over cumin seeds, cloves, cinnamon and bay leaves.

8. Stir in the asafoetida. Reduce flame, add the yoghurt. Stir on low flame till the gravy starts boiling.

9. Add 16 fl oz/2 cups of the reserved liquid, bring to boil and simmer for 5 minutes.

10. Add the gatte and simmer for 10 minutes. Add remaining mint, green chillies and garam masala.

Tips

Time	To Serve
Preparation: 1 hour	Garnish with chopped coriander leaves. Serve hot with roti
Cooking: 30 minutes	

PAPAD KI SABZI

*Poppadams, which are normally served as accompaniments are
turned into a tasty curry.*

Ingredients

Urad daal papad		Cumin (*jeera*) powder	¼ oz/1 tsp
(poppadams), roasted	6 small	Garlic paste	1 oz/2 tbs
Asafoetida (*heeng*)	⅛ oz/½ tsp	Ginger paste	1 oz/2 tbs
Bay leaves (*tej patta*)	2	Onions, chopped	2½ oz/⅓ cup
Cloves	4	Red chilli powder	½ oz/1 tbs
Cooking oil	2½ fl oz/⅓ cup	Salt to taste	
Coriander leaves, chopped	¼ oz/1 tsp	Tomatoes, chopped	2 oz/¼ cup
Coriander powder	½ oz/1 tbs	Turmeric (*haldi*) powder	¼ oz/1 tsp

---

Method

1. Heat oil in a kadhai, add cloves and bay leaves.

2. Dissolve asafoetida in 2 teaspoons water and add to the oil.

3. Stir in chopped onions and sauté till golden brown. Add the ginger and garlic pastes. Stir for 30 seconds, add coriander powder, red chilli powder, salt and turmeric.

4. Stir-cook till the oil separates.

5. Add the chopped tomatoes and cook for a further 2 minutes. Add 24 fl oz/3 cups water and let gravy simmer for 10 minutes on slow fire.

6. Strain into another pan.

7. Break papads into quarters and add to gravy. Add cumin powder then boil for 30 seconds.

Tips

Time	To Serve
Preparation: 30 minutes	Sprinkle with chopped green coriander
Cooking: 30 minutes	and serve hot

PALAK KOFTA

Spinach dumplings in a gravy.

Ingredients

For gravy

Cashew nut paste	1 oz/2 tbs
Cream	½ fl oz/1 tbs
Coriander leaves, chopped	¼ oz/1 tsp
Cumin (*jeera*) seeds	⅛ oz/½ tsp
Garlic paste	¼ oz/1 tsp
Ginger paste	¼ oz/1 tsp
Oil	1 fl oz/2 tbs
Onion, chopped	1 medium
Salt to taste	
Tomatoes, chopped	8¾ oz/1 cup
Turmeric (*haldi*) powder	⅛ oz/½ tsp
Red chilli powder	¼ oz/1 tsp

For koftas

Spinach	6 oz
Gram flour (*besan*)	8¾ oz/1 cup
Cashew nuts, broken	1 oz/2 tbs
Coriander powder	⅛ oz/½ tsp
Cumin (*jeera*) powder	⅛ oz/½ tsp
Oil for frying	
Poppy (*khus khus*) seeds	½ oz/1 tbs
Red chilli powder	⅛ oz/½ tsp
Salt to taste	

Method

To make koftas

1. Clean, wash and par boil spinach leaves. Cool, then squeeze out as much water from the spinach as possible and mash.

2. Grind poppy seeds and cashew nuts to a paste.

3. Except oil, mix all remaining ingredients for the koftas with the paste and spinach.

4. Divide mixture into 8 portions. Form balls by rolling each portion between the palms. Heat oil in a kadhai and deep fry the balls. Keep aside.

For gravy

1. Heat 2 tablespons oil in a kadhai. Splutter cumin seeds. Add chopped onions and brown. Add ginger and garlic pastes, cashew nut paste, turmeric, red chilli powder and salt. Fry for 2-3 minutes.

2. Add chopped tomatoes and fry for another 8-10 minutes. Add 4 fl oz/½ cup water and simmer.

3. Before serving add the koftas to the gravy and simmer for a few minutes.

Tips

Time
Preparation: 15 minutes
Cooking: 20 minutes

To Serve
Pour into a serving bowl. Garnish with coriander leaves and cream

PANEER TAWA MASALA

This is a unique preparation of cottage cheese cooked on a griddle.

Ingredients

Cottage cheese (*paneer*), cubed	1 lb	Ginger juliennes	¼ oz/1 tsp
Black cumin		Ginger paste	¾ oz/4 tsp
(*shah jeera*) seeds	⅛ oz/½ tsp	Green chillies, chopped	2
Carom (*ajwain*) seeds	a pinch	Oil	1½ fl oz/3 tbs
Capsicum, diced	4 oz/½ cup	Oil to fry the cheese	
Coriander powder	¼ oz/1 tsp	Onions, chopped	6 oz/¾ cup
Coriander leaves, chopped	½ oz/1 tbs	Red chilli powder	¼ oz/1 tsp
Cumin (*jeera*) seeds	¼ oz/1 tsp	Salt to taste	
Garam masala	a pinch	Tomatoes, chopped	6 oz/¾ cup
Garlic paste	¾ oz/4 tsp	White pepper powder	¼ oz/1 tsp

Method

1. Heat oil in a kadhai and fry the cottage cheese to golden.

2. Heat the griddle. Add 3 tablespoons oil. When oil is hot add cumin and splutter.

3. Add the chopped onions and brown. Add ginger and garlic pastes, green chillies, coriander powder, red chilli powder, white pepper powder, salt and carom seeds. Fry on medium heat.

4. Add chopped tomatoes. Fry till the oil surfaces.

5. Mix in the cottage cheese, capsicum, garam masala, black cumin and cook for 5 minutes.

Time
Preparation: 10 minutes
Cooking: 15 minutes

To Serve
Garnish with chopped coriander and ginger juliennes. Serve hot with any Indian bread

COCONUT BURFEE

Coconut fudge popular all over India.

Ingredients

Coconut powder	1½ lb/2½ cups	Saffron	a few strands
Cardamom powder	¼ oz/1 tsp	Sugar	2 oz/¼ cup
Pistachios/Silver		Sweet ittar	1 drop
leaf for garnishing	a few	Water	2½ fl oz/⅓ cup

Method

1. Put sugar and water to heat in a pan. Stir continuously till the sugar is completely dissolved.
2. Bring to boil. Add coconut powder, sweet ittar, saffron and cardamom powder. Mix well.
3. Remove from fire and spread evenly on a greased baking tray. Cool and cut into 8 pieces.

Time	To Serve
Preparation: 10 minutes Cooking: 10 minutes	Garnish with pistachios or silver leaf

SERVES: 4

KULFI

Home made ice-cream, rich and distinctive.

Ingredients

Milk	32 fl oz/4 cups	Saffron	a few strands
Cardamom, crushed	1	Sugar	6 oz/¾ cup
Pistachios, blanched and sliced	¼ oz/1 tsp		

Method

1. Put milk and sugar into a large heavy bottomed pan and boil until reduced to a third and mixture is thick and creamy.
2. Add cardamom, pistachio slices and saffron. Cook for 5 minutes. Cool to room temperature.
3. Spoon the mixture into 4 moulds. Tightly cover the moulds with foil and freeze overnight.

Time	To Serve
Preparation: 15 minutes plus 6-7 hours for setting. Cooking: 30 minutes.	Wrap moulds in a warm towel for 5 minutes then invert onto individual serving plates

SERVES: 4

MOONG DAAL HALWA

Ground and fried lentils are turned into a delicious sweet dish.

Ingredients

Lentils (*moong daal*)	4 oz/½ cup	Cardamoms	2
Cashew nuts, broken	¼ oz/1 tsp	Clarified butter (*ghee*)	1 oz/2 tbs
Khoya, fresh, grated	2 oz/¼ cup	Pistachios, chopped	10
Sugar	2 oz/¼ cup	Water	4 fl oz/½ cup

Method

1. Wash and soak the lentils for 30 minutes. Drain out water and grind into a rough paste.
2. Heat ghee in a kadhai and fry the lentil paste till light golden in color.
3. Put the sugar and water to boil in another pan. Stir continuously till the sugar dissolves completely. Boil rapidly for 5 minutes. Add to the fried daal.
4. Cook, stirring vigorously till the mixture becomes thick. Add cardamom powder.

ٹِپ

Time
Preparation: 40 minutes
Cooking: 20 minutes

To Serve
Garnish with khoya, cashew nuts and pistachios. Serve hot

SAFFRON PHIRNI

This ground rice pudding is flavored with pistachios, vetiver and saffron.

Ingredients

Full cream milk	32 fl oz/4 cups	Saffron	a few strands
Rice	2 oz/¼ cup	Sugar	5 oz/⅔ cup
Cardamom powder	¼ oz/1 tsp	Vetiver (*kewda*)	2 drops
Pistachio slivers	¾ oz/4 tsp	4 unglazed earthenware bowls	

Method

1. Wash earthen bowls under running water then soak in water overnight. Drain, wash, and keep aside.

2. Wash the rice thrice and soak for 2 hours.

3. Drain the rice and make a fine paste in a blender using a little water.

4. Soak the saffron in 2 tablespoons of warm water then mash.

5. Heat milk in a thick bottomed pan. Once it boils, remove from heat and add the rice paste. Whip continuosly to prevent lumps.

6. Return to heat and simmer for about 3 minutes.

7. Add the sugar and continue cooking for 2-3 minutes. Remove from heat and strain, while hot, though a soup strainer.

8. Cool the strained rice pudding, stirring occasionally to prevent a skin forming on the surface.

9. Add the cardamom powder, vetiver, saffron (reserving a little for garnish) and stir. Pour into earthenware bowls. Allow to set.

Time
Preparation: 2 hours
Cooking: 10 minutes

To Serve
Sprinkle with pistachio slivers and the reserved saffron. Chill in the refrigerator for at least one hour before serving

KHEER

This ever popular pudding has rice cooked on a slow fire in sweetened milk to make a rich, creamy dish.

Ingredients

Milk	32 fl oz/4 cups	Milk to dissolve saffron	1 fl oz /2 tbs
Rice, long grain	2 oz/¼ cup	Raisins	¼ oz/1 tsp
Almonds	½ oz/1 tbs	Saffron	a few strands
Cardamom powder	¼ oz/1 tsp	Sugar	4 oz/½ cup
Clarified butter (*ghee*)	¼ oz/1 tsp		

Method

1. Wash and soak rice for an hour.

2. Blanch almonds. Remove the skin and cut into slivers.

3. Dissolve the saffron in warm milk and keep aside.

4. Boil milk in a handi.

5. In another handi heat the clarified butter, add rice and stir-cook for 4-5 minutes till it begins to brown lightly.

6. Add the milk and bring to boil, stirring constantly to prevent rice from sticking. Reduce heat and simmer till rice is cooked.

7. Stir in the sugar. Simmer till milk thickens.

8. Stir in cardamom powder, raisins and almonds.

Tips

Time
Preparation: 1 hour
Cooking: 1½ hours

To Serve
Remove to a silver or white metal bowl. Sprinkle saffron and serve hot in winter and cold in summer

SERVES: 4

GAJRELA

Grated carrots cooked in thickened milk garnished with nuts and raisins.

Ingredients

Carrots, grated	2.2 lb	Almonds, blanched and split	¾ oz/4 tsp	Khoya, grated	2 oz
Milk	32 fl oz/4 cups	Clarified butter (ghee)	3½ oz/7 tbs	Raisins	½ oz/1 tbs
				Sugar	8¾ oz/1 cup

Method

1. Boil milk in a kadhai. Add the grated carrots and cook on medium heat, stirring constantly until the milk has thickened.

2. Stir in sugar and cook till most of the moisture has evaporated.

3. Add the ghee and stir-cook for 5 minutes.

4. Remove from fire and mix in the khoya.

Tip

Time
Preparation: 30 minutes
Cooking: 1 hour

To Serve
Garnish with almonds and raisins and silver leaf, if desired. Serve hot

SERVES: 4

GULAB JAMUM

Dried milk dumplings, deep fried and soaked in sugar syrup make a favorite Indian sweet.

Ingredients

Khoya	10¾ oz/1¼ cups	Rosewater	2 drops/4 tbsp
Cardamoms, pealed	5	Saffron	a few strands
Chhena	2 oz/¼ cup	Soda bi-carb	a pinch
Clarified butter (*ghee*) to deep fry		Sugar	34 oz/4 cups
Flour	1½ oz/3 tbs		

Method

1. Knead khoya and chhena gently together.
2. Dissolve soda bi-carb in 1 teaspoon water.
3. Add flour and soda to the khoya and chhena mixure. Knead to a smooth, soft, dough-like consistency.
4. Make 24 balls and smoothen by rolling between your palms.
5. Boil sugar in 16 fl oz/2 cups water for 5-7 minutes till the syrup turns golden brown.
6. Pound saffron. Mix with cardamom seeds and rosewater concentrate to form the filling.
7. Flatten balls. Place a pinch of this filling in the centre, seal and roll into balls again.
8. In a kadhai heat ghee to medium heat. Slide the balls, a few at a time, into the ghee then gently shake the pan till the balls rise to the surface.
9. Remove with slotted spoon and immediately immerse in syrup.

Time
Preparation: 30 minutes
Cooking: 1 hour.
To Serve
Remove to a bowl alongwith syrup and serve hot

MINT RELISH

*A fresh, green, tangy relish that is **Pudina ki Chudney** for you.*

Ingredients

Mint leaves	2 oz/¼ cup	Green chilli	1
Coriander leaves	4 oz/½ cup	Raw mango, chopped	1 oz/2 tbs
Cumin (*jeera*) seeds	¼ oz/1 tsp	Salt to taste	
Garlic cloves	2	Tomatoes, chopped	1½ oz/3 tbs

1. Clean, wash and chop coriander and mint. Slit and deseed green chillies.
2. Blend all ingredients in a food processor.

Note
As mint discolores fast, the proportion of coriander must be kept high

Time
Preparation: 20 minutes

To Serve
Juice of 1 lemon may be added to make the chutney tart.

SERVES: 4

SAUNTH

A sweet and sour relish that complements many Indian dishes.

Ingredients

Dry mango powder (*amchur*)	¾ oz/4 tsp	Raisins	¼ oz/1 tsp
Black pepper powder	⅛ oz/½ tsp	Red chilli powder	⅛ oz/½ tsp
Black salt, powdered	⅛ oz/½ tsp	Salt to taste	
Garam masala	⅛ oz/½ tsp	Sugar	2½ oz/5 tbs
Ginger powder	⅛ oz/½ tsp		

Method

1. Clean and wash the raisins. Keep aside.
2. Mix all the remaining ingredients with 3 fl oz water in a saucepan and cook gently for 15 minutes. Ensure that no lumps remain and the sugar has dissolved. Add raisins.

Time
Preparation: 10 minutes
Cooking: 20 minutes

To Serve
Remove and cool. Serve at room temperature

BHURAANI RAITA

SERVES: 4

Spiced yoghurt is an easy and quick accompaniment to all biryanies.

Ingredients

Yoghurt	1½ lb/2½ cups	
Cumin (*jeera*) powder	⅛ oz/½ tsp	
Garlic, crushed	¼ oz/1 tsp	
Red chilli powder	⅛ oz/½ tsp	
Salt to taste		

Method

1. Rub crushed garlic with salt.
2. Add to yoghurt and whip.
3. Reserve a bit of the chilli and cumin powders and mix the rest into the yoghurt.
4. Pour into a serving bowl. Sprinkle the reserved cumin and chilli in a decorative design on the yoghurt.

SERVES: 4

MIXED RAITA

A delicious yoghurt accompaniment to both vegetarian and non-vegetarian meals.

Ingredients

Yoghurt	1½ lb/2½ cups	Green chilli, finely chopped	¼ oz/1 tsp
Black peppercorns	⅛ oz/½ tsp	Mint, chopped	¼ oz/1 tsp
Chilli powder to sprinkle	a pinch	Onions, chopped	1 oz/2 tbs
Coriander seeds	¼ oz/1 tsp	Salt to taste	
Cucumber, chopped	1 oz/2 tbs	Tomatoes, chopped	1 oz/2 tbs
Cumin (*jeera*) seeds	¼ oz/1 tsp		

Method

1. Heat a griddle and broil cumin, coriander seeds and pepper till dark and aromatic.
2. Pound and keep aside.
3. Whip yoghurt with salt. Add and mix all chopped items.
4. Pour into a glazed earthenware bowl.

Sprinkle with chilli powder and the pounded masalas.

Note
2 oz/4 tablespoons squeezed pineapple chunks can be added for variation.

Tips

Time	**To Serve**
Preparation: 30 minutes	Chill before serving

SERVES: 4

SAMBHAR

A spicy and sour lentil curry.

Ingredients

Green drumsticks, chopped roughly	½ lb	Green chillies, slit	4
Lentils (*toor daal*)	8¾ oz/1 cup	Groundnut/peanut oil	1½ fl oz/3 tbs
Asafoetida (*beeng*)	a pinch	Jaggery	¼ oz/1 tsp
Black lentils (*urad daal*)	¼ oz/1 tsp	Mustard (*sarson*) seeds	¼ oz/1 tsp
Coconut paste	2½ oz/5 tbs	Onions, sliced	6 oz/¾ cup
Coconut water	1 fl oz/2 tbs	Red chilli powder	¼ oz/1 tsp
Coriander leaves, chopped	¾ oz/4 tsp	Salt to taste	
Coriander seeds	¼ oz/1 tsp	Sesame (*til*) seeds	⅛ oz/½ tsp
Cumin (*jeera*) seeds	¼ oz/1 tsp	Tamarind (*imlee*) pulp	½ oz/3 tsp
Curry leaves	15	Tomatoes, quartered	10¾ oz/1¼ cups
		Turmeric (*baldi*) powder	¼ oz/1 tsp

Method

1. Wash and soak toor daal for 30 minutes.
2. Meanwhile dissolve tamarind in 1 fl oz/2 tablespoons water.
3. Pound the jaggery brown sugar and soak in 1 fl oz/2 tablespoons coconut water.
4. Wash and pat dry black lentils. Wash and pat dry curry leaves.
5. Drain toor daal and put in a handi. Add 32 fl oz/4 cups water, green drumsticks, turmeric, red chillies, green chilli powder, onions, tomatoes and salt. Boil, stirring ocassionally till the daal is cooked. Add 1 tablespoon oil and remove from fire.
6. Heat the rest of the oil in a large kadhai, add mustard, sesame, cumin and coriander seeds and the black lentils. Sauté over medium heat till seeds begin to crackle. Add curry leaves, then stir in the asafoetida.
7. Add the cooked daal and tamarind to this tempering. Simmer for 5 minutes.
8. Add the jaggery brown sugar and bring to a boil.
9. Reduce flame, add coconut paste and simmer for 5 minutes more. Sprinkle chopped coriander and stir.

Note
Can be cooked without green drumsticks too.

Tips

Time
Preparation: 1 hour
Cooking: 45 minutes

To Serve
Serve as an accompaniment to boiled rice, dosa and idli. For recipes see pp. 8 and 11